BUILDING TRUST
A Manager's Guide for Business Success

Mary Galbreath Shurtleff, M.A., M.I.M.

A FIFTY-MINUTE™ SERIES BOOK

CRISP PUBLICATIONS, INC.
Menlo Park, California

BUILDING TRUST
A Manager's Guide for Business Success

Mary Galbreath Shurtleff, M.A., M.I.M.

CREDITS
Managing Editor: **Kathleen Barcos**
Editor: **Janis Paris**
Production: **Barbara Atmore**
Typesetting: **ExecuStaff**
Cover Design: **Carol Harris**

Copyright © 1998 by Crisp Publications, Inc.
Printed in the United States of America by Bawden Printing Company.
http://www.crisp-pub.com

Distribution to the U.S. Trade:

National Book Network, Inc.
4720 Boston Way
Lanham, MD 20706
1-800-462-6420

Library of Congress Catalog Card Number 97-77977
Galbreath Shurtleff, Mary
Building Trust for Business Success
ISBN 1-56052-514-2

10 9 8 7 6 5 4 3 2 1

This book is printed on recyclable paper with soy ink.

LEARNING OBJECTIVES FOR:

BUILDING TRUST

The objectives for *Building Trust* are listed below. They have been developed to guide you, the reader, to the core issues covered in this book.

Objectives

❏ 1) To explain the concepts of trust, credibility and mutual understanding.

❏ 2) To show the benefits of trust to an organization.

❏ 3) To provide strategies for encouraging trust and understanding.

Assessing Your Progress

In addition to the Learning Objectives, Crisp, Inc. has developed an **assessment** that covers the fundamental information presented in this book. A twenty-five item, multiple choice/true-false questionnaire allows the reader to evaluate his or her comprehension of the subject matter. An answer sheet with a summary matching the questions to the listed objectives is also available. To learn how to obtain a copy of this assessment please call: **1-800-442-7477** and ask to speak with a Customer Service Representative.

ABOUT THE AUTHOR

Mary Galbreath Shurtleff, owner of Las Vegas-based *Training for Results*, offers a combination of nearly 20 years of management experience and master's degrees in business and the humanities. Mary specializes in helping clients improve customer service and management effectiveness on-site, along with follow-up video training programs.

Before opening her own business, Mary headed training departments for a major utility company, a large financial institution, and the Tropicana Hotel. She is a past president of the Las Vegas Chapter of the American Society for Training and Development, served as Secretary/Treasurer for the Society for Human Resource Management's Consultants Forum, was a member of SHRM's National Training and Development Committee for four years, and has received many professional awards. The author of management articles published in national and international magazines, Mary is also a volunteer at Nathan Adelson Hospice. Her Web site is *trainingforresults.com*.

ABOUT THE SERIES

With over 200 titles in print, the acclaimed Crisp 50-Minute™ series presents self-paced learning at its easiest and best. These comprehensive self-study books for business or personal use are filled with exercises, activities, assessments, and case studies that capture your interest and increase your understanding.

Other Crisp products, based on the 50-Minute books, are available in a variety of learning style formats for both individual and group study, including audio, video, CD-ROM, and computer-based training.

CONTENTS

DEDICATION

This book is dedicated to Marty Shurtleff, Glenn Galbreath, Mr. and Mrs. Frank Spatgen, Jeanne Corcoran, and Nathan Adelson Hospice.

C H A P T E R

I

What Does Trust Mean?

YOUR DEFINITION OF TRUST

1. What does the word "trust" mean for you?

_____

_____

_____

_____

_____

_____

2. What other words do you associate with the concept of "trust"?

Word   *How I connect that word with "trust"*

_____   _____

_____   _____

_____   _____

_____   _____

_____   _____

_____   _____

WHAT IS TRUST?

The concept of "trust" may, at first glance, seem too abstract to be an effective business strategy. Many organizations, however, do recognize the value of building commitment among employees and customers as a practical method to improve the bottom line.

Commitment and trust are inseparable! As the foundation for success, building trust with your employees and your customers creates loyalty, lower turnover, repeat business, and wonderful word-of-mouth advertising.

Although "trust" seems like a simple word, defining it requires some thought. Your own personal definition of trust comes from your experiences, values, and beliefs. What does the word "trust" mean for you?

A DEFINITION OF TRUST

According to *The American Heritage Dictionary*, trust, as a verb, is:

1. To have confidence in: feel sure of

2. To expect with assurance; assume

3. To believe . . .

How do those ideas compare with your own definition and word association? Trust can be an active verb, something you *do*, rather than something you *think about.*

Trust is also a noun, an action. *The American Heritage Dictionary* continues its definition:

1. Firm reliance on the integrity, ability, or character of a person or thing

2. Confident belief

3. Faith

Let's look at the origin of a few of those words which the dictionary uses to define the noun "trust."

INTEGRITY

What role does integrity play in the act of trusting? Coming from the Latin word *intergritas,* the word has, as its root, "integer" or the concept of "whole." The Middle English and Old French definitions include words like completeness, unity, and purity.

When you trust someone or something, you "integrate" them, their ideas, or their actions with yours. When another person trusts you, they accept what you and your organization say and do as genuine.

A DEFINITION OF TRUST (continued)

BELIEF

To believe is "to accept as true or real," according to *The American Heritage Dictionary*. The idea of "truth" or "true" also appears in the dictionary's definition of "belief," which is the mental acceptance or conviction in the truth or actuality of something and "faith," which is the confident belief in the truth, value, or trustworthiness of a person, idea, or thing.

Belief, faith, integrity, and truth are characteristics associated with the idea of trust. Those words, often associated with philosophy or theology, mean bottom line business sense for you.

> *Trust, then, is a choice each person makes to believe someone or something.*

As you build trust with your internal and external customers, you encourage them to believe that you'll do what you say you'll do and that you actually carry out the advertised "image" your organization presents to the public. Internal customers, of course, are your fellow workers; external customers are those who use your products or services.

When others have confidence in you and in your organization, your word-of-mouth advertising and your repeat business increase dramatically. Employee commitment grows as your image becomes internal as well as external. When your company "walks the walk and talks the talk" by treating employees with the same high degree of respect accorded to external customers, you build loyalty among all team members.

WHAT TRUST IS AND IS NOT

What trust is:

Trust is believing that words mean what they appear to mean.

Trust is experiencing actions that are consistent with the verbal or written message.

Trust is having faith that people and the organization as a whole will do what they say they'll do: "credibility of actions"!

What trust is not:

Trust is not trying to "con" others into believing that you're something that you're not.

Trust is not being gullible by believing anything that anyone says is automatically true.

What other words could you add to this list of what trust is and what trust isn't?

_____

_____

_____

EXERCISE 2: *Who Do You Trust?*

Complete the following:

1. Companies/people I trust

    _____

    _____

    _____

    Why I trust them

    _____

    _____

    _____

2. Companies/people I don't trust

    _____

    _____

    _____

    Why I don't trust them

    _____

    _____

    _____

3. Put a **Y** below on those people or companies you trust, and mark those you do not with an **N**.

    ____ Business advisors (mentors, leaders)

    ____ Car dealers

    ____ Colleagues

    ____ Insurance companies

    ____ Team members in personal and professional life (co-workers, volunteer teams, sports, etc.)

    ____ Tobacco companies

    ____ Family

    ____ Friends

    ____ Financial advisors (accountant, financial planner)

    ____ Clients/customers

    ____ Medical advisors (doctors, chiropractors, etc.)

    ____ Legal advisors

    ____ Religious affiliation

Do you find any trends in your answers? Have you spotted any relationships in which you'd like to have more trust?

Certainly, there are no right or wrong answers on your list of people and organizations you trust. When asked, "Why do you trust that person/organization?" many people respond with comments like "I've worked with her before and she's never let me down," "They do what they say they'll do and follow through," "He seems to know what he's talking about," "I feel comfortable working with them," "I know that she has our best interests at heart," or "That company does what it says it'll do."

TRUST MEANS BUSINESS

To work well with staff members and customers, organizations need to develop:

- Open communication

- Commitment and total participation

- Appropriate leadership

- Flexibility to adapt to change

To succeed, co-workers must understand and trust each other enough to work together to achieve their common goal. As we continue through this book, we'll relate the concept of trust to the many characteristics of effective teams—open communication, commitment, and flexibility.

Research has shown that people who trust each other:

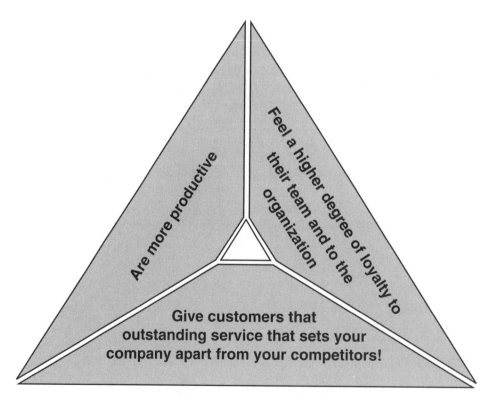

Productivity, loyalty, and outstanding service
have a direct impact on your organization's bottom line!

EXERCISE 3: The "Trustometer"

With 0 degrees as no trust and 100 degrees as perfect trust, please fill in the thermometers listed below to measure your own opinion of the current level of trust in each situation described under a trustometer.

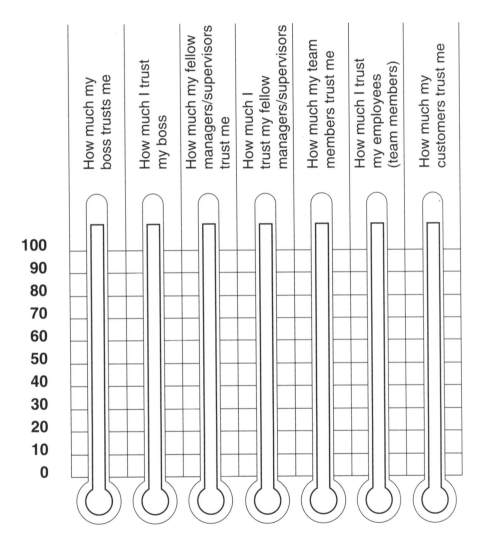

How much my boss trusts me

How much I trust my boss

How much my fellow managers/supervisors trust me

How much I trust my fellow managers/supervisors

How much my team members trust me

How much I trust my employees (team members)

How much my customers trust me

100
90
80
70
60
50
40
30
20
10
0

The "Trustometer"

If you'd like, you may copy and distribute these trustometers to your employees to be returned to you anonymously. Then you can average their answers and do your own team "trustometer."

CHAPTER

II

Foundations of Trust

THREE FUNDAMENTAL INTERPRETATIONS

Trust is often based on interpretations coming from

> ► **INSTINCT**
>
> ► **PAST EXPERIENCE**
>
> ► **CURRENT OBSERVATION/CURRENT EXPERIENCE**

These interpretations acts as "filters" we use to determine whether we'll trust another person or an organization.

INSTINCT

Have you ever just met someone and immediately thought, "Now there's a person I can trust"? What leads you to believe someone you hardly know?

In American culture, behaviors like these usually encourage trust:

- Direct eye contact

- An open facial expression

- Posture indicating interest (leaning forward slightly, nodding)

- A pleasant, confident tone of voice

There's something else, though, that we can't explain away with simple body language or frame of reference. For an undefined reason, on a level that may not be entirely logical, someone or a group simply bonds with us on initial contact. Instinct or "gut reactions" usually can't be explained away by empirical studies. Listening to our instincts is important, even if we don't know where they come from.

EXERCISE 4: *Following Your Instincts*

How often do you follow your instincts about trusting others even if you don't know why you feel the way you do? Answering the questions below will help you rate the role instinct plays in your own judgment.

Please circle the answers that best represent your own experience:

1. I pay attention to my "gut reaction" about someone I don't know very well before I decide on a course of action.

   never   *seldom*   *sometimes*   *often*   *very often*

2. My instincts about people or situations on the job turn out to be correct.

   never   *seldom*   *sometimes*   *often*   *very often*

3. I encourage others to follow their instincts on the job.

   never   *seldom*   *sometimes*   *often*   *very often*

4. I listen when others tell me about their "gut reactions" to work situations.

   never   *seldom*   *sometimes*   *often*   *very often*

5. I reject my instincts because they're not logical and I don't understand them.

   never   *seldom*   *sometimes*   *often*   *very often*

Your answers to Exercise 4 should show you how you feel about your "gut reactions" in business. Although you certainly shouldn't disregard logic, reason, and analysis all the time, remember that your instincts, too, may be sending you an important message about whether or not you should trust someone.

PAST EXPERIENCE

If you're dealing with someone or an organization that you already know, the experience you've had with them in the past helps determine whether you're willing to trust them. The key question to ask yourself when considering past experience is "Did this person/organization do what they said they would do?"

Think back to Exercise 2 where you listed people you did or did not trust. You probably have an example of someone who didn't follow through with what they said they would do. Overpromising and underdelivering destroy trust because the resulting actions don't match the words.

This is called *"credibility of actions."* It's hard to believe that an organization will do what they say they'll do in the future if they've let you down in the past. Credibility of actions means doing what you say you'll do and treating others as you'd like them to treat you and your customers.

EXAMPLE: *Ordering Equipment*

Doing what you say you'll do translates into the concept we call "credibility of actions," a foundation for trust. For example, suppose that you buy computers for your organization from a certain vendor. Three months ago, you ordered five computers for your staff and the vendor promised delivery in two weeks. You received the computers a week after your order.

Did the vendor "deliver" on their promise? Yes, in fact you got the computers early, which most likely exceeded your expectations. You're getting ready to place another order for computer equipment and the vendor tells you you'll have your material within ten days. Do you trust the vendor? Past experience leads you to take the vendor's word because the vendor's "credibility of actions" inspires trust.

If you didn't do what you said you'd do, rebuilding trust becomes difficult. Convincing a customer that this time will be different because you will follow through and meet the deadline is hard because of your customer's past experience with you. Picking up the pieces after you've let someone down is much tougher than reinforcing your "credibility of actions" by doing what you say you'd do in the first place.

EXAMPLE: Using Suggestions

You've recently asked members of your team for specific suggestions on how to improve your department's speed of service. One team member in particular responded enthusiastically with three suggestions. You know that you can't use two of the three ideas, so instead of giving the team member feedback on the ideas, you don't say anything and hope that the team member will forget about the whole thing.

What happens to the trust you're building with your team if you ask for suggestions and don't follow through with feedback on the ideas you receive? When you ask for suggestions, team members then expect you to at least tell them whether or not you'll use their ideas. If you don't say anything, you'll be falling below their expectations; you won't be doing what you've "said" that you'd do.

Trust goes out the window when you ask for ideas and don't follow up on them. Does that mean that you must use every idea you receive? Absolutely not! Most people don't expect you to use every single suggestion that they make. They do, however, expect your comments on their ideas.

If you ignore what they've said, you send the message that you're really just going through the motions and aren't interested in their suggestions. You break the trust. The next time you ask your team for ideas, they won't trust you enough to give you the time of day.

Trust and Service Recovery

Turning customer problems into opportunities is one way to keep customers coming back. In fact, business publications have already coined a buzzword to describe just that process—"service recovery."

If you or your company disappoint a customer, chances are that you've damaged your credibility of actions—the fact that you'll do what you say you'll do. Your image suffers when you advertise high quality and special treatment and fail to deliver on your promises. Customers won't trust you the next time they're ready to spend their money because your actions and words don't match!

PAST EXPERIENCE (continued)

EXERCISE 5: The Case of the Complaint Letter

Let's look at a real-world case ripe for service recovery. After you read through the case, ask yourself how you would have reacted if this were your business.

Several years ago a couple spent their anniversary at one of their favorite hotels in California. They'd saved all year to splurge on a luxurious room. Everything seemed to go wrong during their stay. The cocktail servers were extremely slow and seemed to ignore them. Their room overlooked the parking lot, which was noisy all day and night with construction and guests.

One night a band played in an open air gazebo right next to their room until midnight. In their room, they noticed a tent card encouraging guests to write directly to the general manager if they had compliments or concerns about their stay.

The couple paid their bill, and went on their way. When they returned home, they wrote a letter to the general manager detailing factually what had happened to them and how disappointed they were in their favorite hotel. They did not ask for any kind of reimbursement or special consideration.

What would you do if, as a general manager, you received a letter like that about your organization?

_____

_____

_____

_____

_____

_____

_____

Turning a Problem into an Opportunity

The general manager wrote back a cold, extremely defensive letter stating that the cocktail service couldn't possibly have been slow at the hotel, that the parking lot construction had to continue at night so the hotel could meet their deadline for remodeling, and that the open air band had been a private party which netted a great deal of revenue for the hotel.

Not once did the general manager apologize or acknowledge that the couple had valid concerns. Will the couple trust this hotel enough to spend over a thousand dollars there again for a special occasion? No!

How do you turn a complaint like that into an opportunity? Certainly not by becoming defensive and refusing to consider that perhaps your company has a problem! To rebuild trust with the couple, the general manager should:

1. Apologize for the difficult situation.

2. Thank the customers for bringing the matter to the company's attention.

3. Work toward a solution. Perhaps ask the customers what the company can do to satisfy them. Or offer the customers something complimentary—10% off their room rate for their next stay, free parking, or a complimentary cocktail. The company doesn't have to "give away the store" to make up for negative experience.

4. Invite the customers back and assure them that their experience will be more positive the next time.

By showing the customers that the company took their complaints seriously and cared about their disappointment, the general manager practices service recovery. Re-establishing trust with customers through service recovery encourages repeat business and promotes great word-of-mouth advertising.

What are trust and service recovery methods your company could implement?

PAST EXPERIENCE (continued)

EXERCISE 6: Create an Atmosphere of Trust for Your Customers

Creating an atmosphere of trust for customers is important. To show customers that you have confidence in the quality of your service, try these techniques:

Guarantees

Draft a simple "money back" guarantee that tells your customers that you'll refund their money if they aren't satisfied. Of course, you'll want to consult with your legal and financial advisors for the wording of any kind of guarantee or refund arrangement.

Items that should appear on guarantee:

_____

_____

If a "money back" guarantee doesn't apply to your organization, you may want to consider the alternative of offering to fix problems to the customer's satisfaction. In either case, include a method where you can track specifically why the customer was dissatisfied.

Points at which you could check satisfaction:

_____

_____

Customer Feedback

Show customers that you trust them by asking for their feedback and using their ideas whenever possible. Customers will feel like you value their input if you ask them for ratings or comments on your products and services.

CURRENT EXPERIENCE

Sometimes, though, you don't have any past experience to guide you. Your decision to trust is based on your impression of a person or an organization right now. Advertising sends us messages to encourage us to trust their slogans and buy their products or services. Companies spend millions of dollars on "image advertising" to convince us that we'll have a positive experience if we do business with them. What happens to those advertising dollars when our own impression of the business doesn't match the advertised image?

Do the Messages Match?

Messages and impressions must match for us to trust a company enough to spend our money with them. All the advertising in the world can't make up for poor service or products that don't meet quality standards.

EXAMPLE: *Image Versus Reality*

Advertising

Company X takes out a full page ad in the newspaper to announce its new customer service program, "Put Service First." The ad features catchy slogans about their prompt, friendly staff, along with lots of pictures of smiling workers and happy customers.

So far, so good. But what if a customer walks into Company X and:

- No one even makes eye contact with him when he walks by?
- No one acknowledges him at all or thanks him if he makes a purchase?

"Put Service First" rapidly becomes "Put Service Last" because, in spite of its glowing advertising campaign, Company X doesn't follow through with "credibility of actions." Although the customer reads Company X's ads and decides he likes what he sees, he soon finds out that he can't trust Company X to live up to its advertising.

Will customers come back to Company X? No! Company X's ads and their own experience don't match. For Company X to be as good as it says it is, X has to build trust with its customers and employees.

CURRENT EXPERIENCE (continued)

Effective teams share common goals, mutual understanding, and trust. The only way to be as good as you say you are is to build trust with customers and employees:

1. **Do what you say you'll do.** Don't "overpromise and under-deliver," either with your employees or with your customers.

2. **Create an atmosphere of trust.** Set the example yourself by speaking and acting the way you'd like for your team members to treat your customers and each other. Insist upon open, direct communication.

3. **Trust your team members** by developing and communicating standards which give them the power to take care of customers in ordinary situations.

4. **Appreciate positive results.** Thank customers for their business. Notice good job performance and look for reasons to celebrate!

5. **Ask for input** from your customers and team members through surveys and informal feedback. Use their ideas whenever possible and explain the situation to them if you can't adopt their suggestions.

Orientation

Let's take a look at X's orientation program. Imagine that you've just gone to work for X. During new employee orientation, X's top executive says, "At X, service is our middle name. People are our most important asset. Our employees are the key to our success." As a new staff member, you discover

► Your supervisor never asks for your input on changes and isn't interested in your ideas for improvement.

► All anyone seems to care about is putting in their time and no one from your department ever discusses customer service.

Do you feel like part of Company X's team? As an employee, do you think you're Company X's "most important asset"? Do you trust what you heard in orientation? It takes courage to do what you say you'll do, to trust someone else, and to encourage others to trust you. Building trust, however, makes great "business sense." Can Company X "clean up its act" and live up to its advertising? Of course! By communicating and reinforcing service expectations with all team members, Company X really will "Put Service First"!

The concept of trust may seem too theoretical to be a practical business strategy. Defining standards or expectations and leading by example, however, are practical ways to inspire trust with your internal and external customers.

When you trust another person, a written commitment, a company's image, or a mission statement, you make the choice to believe the message that you're receiving from someone else.

TO TRUST OR NOT TO TRUST

EXERCISE 7: A Present Situation

Our next exercise gives you the opportunity to list a trust issue you're facing and apply the filters of instinct, past, and current experience as you decide whether to trust someone. Think of a situation in your current job where you're not sure you should trust another person—a co-worker, a customer, a boss, another department. Describe that situation below:

_____

_____

_____

_____

_____

Now, using trust filters, try to identify where your doubts concerning this situation come from.

Trust Filters	Yes	No	Wait and See
Instinct:			
Do my instincts tell me to trust this person?	❏	❏	❏
Past Experience:			
Does my past experience lead me to trust this person?	❏	❏	❏
Current Experience:			
Do this person's verbal and nonverbal messages match?	❏	❏	❏
Does what I know about this person match my current impression?	❏	❏	❏

EXERCISE 8: What Would You Do?

Here's a sample situation. Suppose you're considering working with Joe, another manager, on an important project. You don't know Joe very well, so you ask yourself our "trust filter" questions to help you decide whether you want to team up with him.

Trust Filters	Yes	No	Wait and See

Instinct:

Do my instincts tell me to trust this person? ☐ ☐ ☑

You haven't worked with Joe before and don't know him very well so your instincts aren't sending you a clear message. You'll keep an open mind.

Past Experience:

Does my past experience lead me to trust ☑ ☐ ☐
this person?

You've competed with Joe for visibility and recognition in the past. You've both presented separately at meetings asking for approval on different projects. You know, however, that Joe does good work and is well known in the company. Your answer is a cautious "yes."

Current Experience:

Do this person's verbal and nonverbal ☑ ☐ ☐
messages match?

Does what I know about this person match ☑ ☐ ☐
my current impression?

Joe's professional manner seems to be fairly consistent and he has let it be known it is important to him to do a good job.

Joe just approached you and suggested that you work together the next time you have the opportunity. Joe explained that he wants a chance to expand his skills and that he'd like to learn from you, as well as to share ideas with you that would help you in return. Joe gives you a frank assessment of his own strengths and weaknesses and seems very open about what he'd like to learn.

What do you do? Judging from the evidence, you could probably believe him and decide to proceed with caution.

MUTUAL UNDERSTANDING

We often trust people and organizations who connect with us through images, stories, or examples in our own frame of reference. Finding common ground helps us to communicate effectively and develop mutual understanding.

Our "trust filters," then, center on two concepts:

Degree of credibility of actions:

- Do actions match words in the past and in the present?

- Does the person do what he says he'll do?

Degree of mutual understanding:

- Can you communicate with each other effectively?

CASE STUDY: Kokomo

People from different backgrounds or cultures frequently have trouble relating to each other.

Imagine that as an American, you've taken on a project with your company that requires you to work on a team with a group from the mythical country of Kokomo. You've grown up in a culture that values individual accomplishment, free speech, directness, punctuality, and winning. Kokomoans, however, come from a background that stresses modesty, agreement, tact, and team achievement, where being "on time" isn't important. How will you find common ground with such differences? Let's compare and contrast a typical meeting for you and for the Kokomoans.

In your company, a week before a meeting you usually receive an agenda like that shown here. The agenda includes the approximate discussion time allowed for each item. Most meetings last an hour and feature action items to be completed by specified dates. Meetings start and end on time.

Agenda

Sample meeting agenda for your company

Meeting date, time (start and end), place

I. Introduction and updates from the previous meeting (15 minutes)

    A. Review and approval of the minutes from the previous meeting

    B. Report on the status of Project A

    C. Update on Project B

II. Develop time line for new Project C (30 minutes)

    A. Steps necessary for Project C

    B. How Project C fits in with A and B

III. Conclusion: action items for Project C (15 minutes)

    Action: *Person(s) responsible:*   *Completion date:*

Kokomoans don't do an agenda for meetings. If the meeting is supposed to start at 10 A.M., most people get there by 10:30 A.M. Everyone has coffee and chats about their families for about a half an hour. The person who has called the meeting starts things off by asking everyone a general question like "What should we do about Project C?" Then, each person in the room gives his or her opinion at great length.

Eventually, someone suggests a course of action. If everyone agrees with the plan, then the meeting is over. Most of their meetings last at least three hours. Kokomoans wouldn't dream of asking someone to speak for only a certain length of time. That would be rude and would show a lack of respect for the person's opinion.

MUTUAL UNDERSTANDING (continued)

The trust filter that takes center stage when working with people from a different culture is "current experience/observation." It's difficult to rely too much on instinct because your instincts result, in part, from your own culture. Unless you have past experience working with Kokomoans, your frame of reference will get in your way if you try to apply your own values to another culture.

Keeping an open mind and making a concerted effort to establish common ground will help you develop mutual understanding with the Kokomoans.

EXERCISE 9: Establishing Common Ground

Based on the previous description of Kokomo, list similarities and differences you personally would have with the Kokomoans:

Similarities	Differences

Now, how could you establish common ground with the Kokomoans? How could you adapt to their culture while maintaining those features of your own culture that you consider worthwhile?

_____

_____

_____

_____

_____

As you may have noted, your work together on a team will give all of you a common goal, a concept comfortable for the Kokomoans and not entirely new to you. You also share a common language, English, although their vocabulary may differ somewhat. Working through punctuality issues and communication styles (directness versus modesty and a real focus on tact) requires some compromise.

You may, for example, want to do a general agenda. Keeping in mind that the Kokomoans like to start by chatting, you could allow extra time in the introduction to let each person talk about himself or herself. Although you want the meeting to stay on track, you might try asking the Kokomoans what kind of action item list they would prefer to use so each person knows what to do.

How did you use the information you know about Kokomo to better serve your Kokomoan customers? You probably realized that you may need to spend a little extra time with the Kokomoans. The Kokomoans, too, would expect a certain amount of social chatting while doing business with you.

TIPS FOR WORKING ON A TEAM

As managers, we encourage our staff members and our customers to trust us when we determine common ground which helps us communicate more effectively. Explaining how each person's actions affect the team as a whole, for example, establishes common ground among team members.

Here are suggestions for building trust when working on a project with others:

- Share current data on progress toward goals. Post simple charts or graphs on productivity, customer satisfaction, gross sales, or other measurements where team members can see how the team is doing.

- Ask for suggestions and use them or explain why you can't. Follow up on all ideas.

- Ask everyone to explain any obstacles that are keeping them from doing their jobs efficiently. Note their specific comments and act on any items you can.

C H A P T E R

III

Consequences of a Lack of Trust

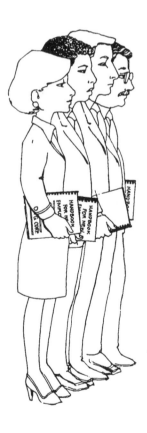

WHY PEOPLE DON'T TRUST

Our corporate culture—and in fact all the beliefs we have about how this country was built—seem to emphasize individualism and competition. Although these characteristics have a valid place, their over-emphasis can lead to a work environment that is neither optimal for the employees nor delivers the best service to clients and customers. In this chapter we examine the negative aspects of a nontrusting work environment as well as the fears that keep us from adopting a trusting environment.

What keeps you from trusting others in the workplace? Why won't others trust you? Trusting someone else can be frightening. After all, if you accept what someone else says as true, you open yourself up to the possibility of deception or vulnerability. What if you trust a co-worker to do a project and he doesn't finish on time? Then you'll be responsible for missing a deadline.

What about your customers? Let's say that in the spirit of trustworthiness, you institute a "service guarantee" where you give your customers their money back if they're not satisfied. Unscrupulous customers might take advantage of you and ask for their money back under false pretenses.

Trusting someone means taking a risk. People often come up with a whole list of reasons why they shouldn't trust anyone else in a business situation. Those obstacles to trust could also be called "Yabuts." You know the phrase, "I'd like to trust them. *Yeah, but* what if . . . ?"

WELL YES, MADAME... BUT WE **DID** REMOVE THE STAIN.

WHY PEOPLE DON'T TRUST (continued)

Here are some common "yabuts" that keep us from trusting each other on the job:

"Yabut . . . what if . . . "

I depend on someone else, they let me down, and I take the fall?

I believe a co-worker, communicate honestly, and then get hurt when that person turns out to be a backstabber?

I share a project with someone and they

—don't do things my way?

—hog all the credit if we succeed?

—blame me if we fail?

—turn out to be better than I am?

I tell my customers that I guarantee their satisfaction and they use that as an excuse to keep from paying us?

These are all valid concerns—go into trust with your eyes wide open. These things will happen occasionally. The consequences, though, of not trusting are much worse.

EXERCISE 10: Me, Trust Someone Else? Yabut . . .

In the space below, list as many objections to trust—"yabuts"—as possible. (Think of the actions you most avoid at work. What are the worst consequences you are imagining?)

"Yabuts" that discourage trust on the job:

1. _____

_____

2. _____

_____

3. _____

_____

4. _____

_____

5. _____

_____

6. _____

_____

7. _____

_____

Has this helped in any way to identify fears that are unfounded? Has this identified any situations that are less fear-invoking than others . . . where you might be more willing to take a chance?

WHAT HAPPENS WHEN YOU DON'T TRUST

Think back to the most effective and enjoyable work experience you ever had. How did the element of trust fit into that picture?

When you compare that to the worst job environment you've experienced, what would you say were the problems that arose in the nontrusting workplace? How did they affect you? Did they seem to spread over time?

Would you say that it was worth taking the risk of a few new behaviors in order to achieve a trusting environment?

A LACK OF TRUST LEADS TO

1. A Lack of Commitment

2. Lower Employee Satisfaction

3. A Lack of Open Communication

4. Empty Words and Unrealistic Images

CONSEQUENCE #1: A LACK OF COMMITMENT

Commitment to a common goal is the foundation for all success. Trust directly influences commitment. Commitment comes from feeling like a part of the organization and sharing in that organization's goals.

If an organization doesn't trust its employees, how can anyone possibly be expected to devote themselves to working at their highest potential toward the betterment of the organization?

Commitment and loyalty come from being *included* rather than *excluded* in decision making and information sharing. How do you think trust relates to commitment? Write down some of your thoughts as you answer the next exercise.

EXERCISE 11: Commitment and Trust

Please complete the following blanks based on your own experience:

1. "I don't feel committed to a common goal when . . . "

_____

_____

_____

2. "To be effective, my employees and I must commit to achieving common goals because . . . "

_____

_____

_____

3. "Commitment is based on trust because . . . "

_____

_____

_____

4. "Trust helps me feel committed because . . . "

_____

_____

_____

5. "To show my commitment to my customers, I need to . . . "

_____

_____

_____

COMMON RESPONSES TO "COMMITMENT AND TRUST" QUERIES

Common answers to issues listed in Exercise 11 are given here:

1. "I don't feel committed to a common goal when . . . "

- I have no about input how the goal is set or how I'll achieve the goal.

- No one even tells us about the goal until it's too late.

- You don't know what progress you're making toward the goal.

When employees don't have any input into the structure or action plan involving goals, naturally they don't feel as committed to achieving the goals. Asking others for ideas and implementing as many of their thoughts as possible means that you trust your team members.

The old style "dictatorial" management of "I'm the boss and you're not" doesn't value others enough to build commitment by using their ideas. To unite everyone toward achieving a goal, you have to trust them enough to ask for and use their feedback as often as possible.

2. "To be effective, my employees and I must commit to achieving common goals because . . . "

- Otherwise, you have a "team" in name only.

- Without common goals, it becomes "every person for him/herself" and only a few achieve their personal goals at the department's expense.

- The bottom line suffers if you and your staff aren't working to the highest capacity.

So many organizations subscribe to the team approach in name only. "If we call you a team, give you a button that says you're a team, and give you time to have team meetings, then you *must be a team*." Nothing could be farther from the truth.

> *If we call you an elephant, give you a button that says you're an elephant, and give you time to go to the zoo, you certainly don't become an elephant!*

COMMON RESPONSES TO "COMMITMENT AND TRUST" QUERIES (continued)

Teams exist to work together. They work together to achieve a goal more effectively and/or efficiently than they could if they worked separately. If the team members don't trust each other, then no matter what you call them, they'll never be a team and they won't achieve the goal you've given them.

3. "Commitment is based on trust because . . . "

Commitment involves actually investing yourself in a job and opening yourself up enough to trust that your work will have an impact. If you don't believe that another person, a department, or an entire organization values your work, you won't feel motivated to "give it your all" and work to your full potential.

4. "Trust helps me feel committed because . . . "

- You know that you can count on others to work *with* you, rather than *against* you.

- You feel you have the power you need to be effective in your job. If your organization or your boss trusts you, you should have the ability to make most of the decisions you need to make, either on your own or working with others.

- You can give your customers the best possible service because you have the power to help them resolve problems or to offer them "something extra."

5. "To show my commitment to customers, I need to . . . "

- Show more interest in customers and develop ways to get their feedback.

- Invest more time in training my employees.

CONSEQUENCE #2: LOWER EMPLOYEE SATISFACTION

There is a direct link between trust and lowered employee morale, lowered productivity, and higher turnover. If your employees don't trust what you say or what messages your organization sends them, then, as we've seen, they won't feel as committed to working up to their full potential. That, of course, adversely affects productivity as you end up with many employees who are working just enough to get by.

Morale also takes a nose-dive if your messages and actions don't match.

> *"People are our most important assets"* may be a fine message for new employee orientation, but if you don't treat employees with respect and don't give them the ability to make as many job-related decisions as possible, then your message isn't true.

Morale and commitment are directly related. Employees who feel like they're part of an organization or that their suggestions have value are much more likely to stay motivated on the job.

Job satisfaction is a major factor in many employees' decision to stay with or to leave a boss or a company. Replacing employees is extremely costly.

High turnover:

- Hurts the bottom line

- Decreases the level of service to customers by constantly relying on employees new to the organization

- Makes it difficult to build a team

THE REVOLVING DOOR SYNDROME

Most people have experienced the "revolving door syndrome" as customers. It's frustrating to go somewhere where no one knows you. You constantly have to explain what you want, even if you've been coming there for a long time, because the new people have no background with you.

Often the new employee doesn't know much about the products or services so it's difficult for him or her to give you good service. Customers want to feel "special," understood, welcome, and at ease.

How can customers develop a relationship with a business if they have to start all over again with a new salesperson or staff member every time? If you have a "revolving door" when it comes to staffing, you lose your team's continuity in working toward a common goal.

EXERCISE 12: The "Revolving Door"

For this exercise, think about your own experiences as a customer.

Describe an actual situation where you, as a customer, constantly had to do business with new staff members at a company because employees wouldn't work there for very long.

_____

_____

_____

_____

1. How did you feel about doing business with that company?

_____

_____

_____

2. From a customer's perspective, how would you describe the atmosphere at that company?

_____

_____

_____

3. How much did the employees know about the company's products and services?

_____

_____

_____

4. How did their level of knowledge affect you as the customer?

_____

_____

_____

CONSEQUENCE #3: A LACK OF OPEN COMMUNICATION

In an atmosphere where everyone has to "watch his/her back," people withhold vital information from each other because "information is power." Withholding information, giving only bits and pieces of the big picture, or misleading others kills any opportunity for the open communication businesses need to achieve peak results.

If workers don't trust each other or if the company doesn't trust its employees enough to share information, the organization ends up with too many decisions made by too few people, those with the power that information brings.

A lack of true communication also flies in the face of what should be one of every organization's core values: honesty. An environment that breeds suspicion ends up stifling good ideas, encouraging infighting and unhealthy competition, and destroying any enthusiasm employees might have about their jobs.

Negative attitudes are contagious—customers, too, can feel when the workforce doesn't care about the organization.

EXERCISE 13: Diagnosis: Lack of Trust

Describe a time when you, as the customer, could tell that employees working for a company where you do business didn't care about their jobs.

1. How could you tell, as a customer, that negative attitudes were contagious at this company?

2. What do you, as a customer, think would have stopped the spread of those negative attitudes? Did you continue to do business there? Why or why not?

Consciously or unconsciously, customers feel when negative thinking spreads throughout a business. That widespread negativity frequently comes from employees who don't trust their employer or each other.

CASE STUDY: The Case of the Muddled Manager

Ms. Z went to every customer service seminar her company offered. She read all the latest books and articles about service excellence because she wanted her team of 30 employees to give all their customers outstanding service.

At her weekly staff meetings, she'd spend at least 10 minutes talking about the importance of service, covering the basics like the importance of greeting customers, making eye contact, using a pleasant tone of voice, and anticipating customers' needs. Yet her own employees didn't seem to practice what Ms. Z was preaching. The service in her department continued to be mediocre at best.

Ms. Z's daily routine went something like this: She'd come into the building, walk quickly by all the employees with no comment, go into her office, and shut the door. Her main contact with employees was her weekly meeting or emergencies which required her immediate attention.

1. Describe the kind of service you would imagine that Ms. Z's employees were giving their customers:

_____

_____

_____

_____

2. Why aren't Ms. Z's staff members giving their customers better service?

_____

_____

_____

_____

CASE STUDY (continued)

3. What should Ms. Z do to help her department's service improve?

_____

_____

_____

_____

4. Your suggestions for Ms. Z's new action plan to improve service:

_____

_____

_____

_____

Unfortunately, the Case of the Muddled Manager is based on an actual situation. So, what do you think is wrong with this picture? Ms. Z deserves kudos for her interest in reading and learning about service, but she fails in the example she sets for her team.

Actions _do_ speak louder than words and Ms. Z's staff members are reflecting the way she treats them. Her employees probably don't greet customers with much enthusiasm and avoid helping customers at all if they can.

Her example says "Don't make eye contact. Don't greet people—in fact, stay away from the frontline as much as you can. Don't initiate a two-way conversation, just tell people what to do." That's why her employees don't listen to or trust her discussions of service. Her own actions don't match her words. Of course, a poor example doesn't always prevent employees from giving good service. The way a manager _acts_, however, sets the tone for the office.

STEPS FOR IMPROVING SERVICE

What did you suggest that Ms. Z do to improve service? Here are some thoughts on a new action plan to help Ms. Z build up her "credibility of actions":

STEP 1   *Greet employees in the morning,* and say "good-bye" at the end of the day when you can.

STEP 2   *Ask employees for specific ideas* during weekly meetings on how to improve service, and implement as many of those ideas as possible. Explain the reason why you can't use any ideas you don't implement.

STEP 3   *Use actual examples* of challenging service situations during the weekly meetings and ask employees what they think is the best way to handle that situation.

STEP 4   *Walk among the employees* and compliment them when they do something right. Don't just talk with employees when there's something wrong.

STEP 5   *Open your office door* when you can and encourage employees to discuss work-related issues with you where appropriate.

If you want your employees to treat your customers with respect and courtesy and listen to them, then they have to trust that you'll model those same behaviors. Those "links" form the service chain: how you treat your employees directly affects how your employees treat your customers.

STEPS FOR IMPROVING SERVICE (continued)

The Challenge to Cooperate

Ms. Z's organization had a reputation for an "us against them" approach to management. Managers viewed themselves on one side and employees felt as if they were on the other side. An ugly incident brought the adversarial relationship to a head, pitting employees against management, and damaging many long-standing working relationships.

Even after the incident was settled, workers and managers didn't trust each other because of the deep scars the trouble had caused. Customers were complaining about poor service and revenues started to drop.

To move ahead with the company and continue to be competitive, employees and management realized that they would have to work together. Ms. Z's organization's labor leaders and management formally agreed to a combined task force called "Project Team."

"PROJECT TEAM"

Simply announcing a joint effort, however, amounted to little more than lip service without the employees and management working together to make the organization successful. The union and executive management each appointed two managers and two employees as leaders for "Project Team." The four task force leaders received training on how to organize and lead meetings, along with skill development on problem solving and follow-up.

What challenges do you think the four "Project Team" leaders faced as they started to form their task force?

_____

_____

_____

_____

_____

_____

_____

In the beginning, the leaders' biggest challenge centered on building trust that "Project Team" would be more than just an exercise in futility.

► *Employees* were skeptical because they thought that management wouldn't really listen to and implement their ideas.

► *Managers* thought that the workers who volunteered to be on the task force would just use the meetings as an excuse to get paid for sitting around.

► *Everyone* was waiting to see how this whole thing would go and not many wanted to be the first to participate.

"PROJECT TEAM" (continued)

What suggestions do you have to help the "Project Team" leaders overcome those challenges?

_____

_____

_____

_____

_____

_____

_____

The leaders put their own reputations behind "Project Team" and did everything they could to encourage employees and management to participate. They had a definite agenda, stayed within scheduled time limits, and focused on defining and implementing ideas that would improve service fairly quickly. The leaders did what they said they'd do, followed up on all ideas, and encouraged the organization to use the task force's suggestions whenever possible.

"Project Team" produced some dramatic results: hundreds of thousands of dollars saved and increased customer satisfaction. A success? Absolutely. A smooth easy transition? Hardly.

There were a few managers who refused to cooperate when the task forces made suggestions in their areas. There were some employees who thought the whole idea was "window dressing" and refused to participate.

The leaders were the key to success, however, because, through their credibility of actions, they built enough trust for managers and employees to develop suggestions together.

"Project Team" and Trust

How did the "Project Team" leaders rebuild trust?

1. *They "trusted" the process* enough to put their own enthusiasm and commitment into encouraging employees and managers to give the project a try. In some cases, they went out to the work site and spent 10 or 20 minutes doing informal training by talking with employees and managers about issues like customer service or the importance of teamwork.

2. *The leaders were honest* about their own ambivalence. They expressed their own skepticism and they also talked about their own willingness to trust the process enough to give the teams a chance.

3. *They made sure that each task force knew the status* of their suggestions and, at first, aimed at completing projects in a relatively short timeframe so the groups could see the results of their suggestions.

Although "Project Team" is a fictional example based on common, real-world situations, restoring trust through credibility of actions by an organization doing what it says it will do is the foundation of rebuilding trust.

CONSEQUENCE #4: EMPTY WORDS AND UNREALISTIC IMAGES

> *Many organizations say "People are our most important asset." Those become empty words, however, if you and your organization don't show your employees that you trust them.*

Let's change that slogan for a minute. Let's imagine that your organization just purchased a computer that is "state of the art"—it tracks customers, allows you to target your marketing, gives you up-to-the-minute revenue figures, sends e-mail worldwide, and provides you with information resources you never dreamed you'd have.

People—The Ultimate Computer

You spent thousands, perhaps millions, of dollars on this computer and have high hopes for its success. In accounting, assets are often "things" like computers or buildings. From a financial standpoint, your company may really be thinking "Our computer is our most important asset." Ask yourself these questions about your computer:

- Do you abuse the computer by beating on it, denting it, yanking wires out of it?

- Do you expect the computer to exceed its capacity without adding memory or software?

- Do you expect the computer to work without any kind of power—i.e., electricity, batteries, solar panels, back-up generators?

You probably answered "No" to each question and may have wondered who in the world would treat an expensive, state-of-the-art computer system that way. Yet, organizations, even those who say "People are our most important asset," often treat their employees in the manner described.

EXERCISE 14: Our Most Important "Asset"?

Ask yourself these questions about the people who are supposed to be your most important asset:

1. Does your organization "abuse" people verbally by tolerating a culture which features yelling at, insulting, and berating employees?

_____

_____

_____

2. Do you expect your employees to perform a new skill or improve on existing behavior without coaching or training?

_____

_____

_____

3. Do you expect employees to work without any kind of positive feedback or recognition when they do a good job?

_____

_____

_____

4. Do you want them to "take care of the customer" without giving them the _power_ to do so?

_____

_____

_____

MAKE PEOPLE YOUR MOST IMPORTANT ASSET!

You treat the computer as an important asset so that the computer will perform optimally. You "trust" that you'll get your ROI (return on investment) for this equipment so you take care of it, adding memory or software as upgrades when necessary. You probably have the computer hooked up to a power source (electricity in most cases) with a surge guard to protect the computer from uneven power flows. If your computer can't keep up with your needs in the future, chances are you will use it in another way.

Employees certainly aren't computers. If you really want to make the "People are our most important asset" slogan come alive, here's what you can do:

1. **Build employees' trust** by treating them fairly and respectfully.

2. **Offer training and coaching** to support employees as your business focus changes or broadens.

3. **Foster a culture** in your organization or at least in your own department where you *do not tolerate verbal abuse* of any kind involving communications between management and employees or co-worker to co-worker.

How can you expect your employees to feel like your most important asset if other employees or managers yell at them and berate them at work? That kind of treatment won't produce the long term results you want and destroys trust in the blink of an eye!

No one likes to fail. As a manager, or a coach, you may be exasperated when your team members try something new and don't succeed. Of course, businesses can't survive if all they do is fail. Giving your staff members the "latitude" to fail, as long as they're using what they consider to be good judgment, goes a long way to building trust. Let's look at the following example.

EXERCISE 15: *Assuming Responsibility*

Supervisor A had been on the job for two weeks in an entertainment facility. One night, when she was the only supervisor working, she had a group of unhappy customers who expected to be paid for a game they were playing because they thought they had won.

Supervisor A checked out the situation and found out that several of the customers had not joined the game in time to be eligible for the winnings. She explained the situation to all the players, but everyone started yelling because the two "late" players insisted they'd played on time and should get part of the winnings.

Supervisor A excused herself, consulted the policy book, and saw that she had the authority, as the only supervisor on duty, to make the decision to pay all those at the table, because the amount of the winnings was under the maximum allowed for her discretion.

What would you do the next day if you were Supervisor A's boss?

_____

_____

_____

_____

_____

How would you help Supervisor A learn to handle that situation in the future?

_____

_____

_____

_____

_____

MAKE PEOPLE YOUR MOST IMPORTANT ASSET! (continued)

This is a tricky situation. You certainly don't want to destroy Supervisor A's confidence by reprimanding her for paying the table. You trusted Supervisor A to be the only management person on duty. Supervisor A consulted policy and made the decision to use her discretion, following guidelines, to pay all the players at the table.

Although you may have handled the situation differently yourself, it's up to you to reinforce the supervisor's attempt to follow procedure and to make a judgment. You certainly have the opportunity to point out other policies or methods to use if this situation comes up again. The quickest way to destroy trust is to jump all over someone who is doing their best to follow guidelines to make a decision on their own.

One of our biggest challenges as managers is to trust our team members enough to use their honest failures as learning opportunities for them. As long as employees don't repeatedly fail or endanger the business, an occasional failure is a great learning experience if the manager gives constructive, instead of destructive, feedback.

CHAPTER

IV

Three Steps for Encouraging Trust

ACTION PLAN FOR ENCOURAGING TRUST

In this chapter we'll look at some concrete steps for implementing your action plan.

> **1.** **STEP ONE:** Ask for input and put it to use.
>
> **2.** **STEP TWO:** Do what you say you'll do.
>
> **3.** **STEP THREE:** Delegate effectively.

STEP ONE: ASK FOR INPUT AND PUT IT TO USE

Show your employees and your customers that you're genuinely open to their ideas by asking for their feedback when you're making major decisions. Ask them how to make things better and listen to their response.

EXERCISE 16: Asking Employees and Customers for Input

To help you plan Step One, please complete the questionnaire listed below.

1. What are you personally doing on the job to ask your team members for input?

   Formally:

   _____

   _____

   _____

   Informally:

   _____

   _____

   _____

2. What are you personally doing on the job to ask your customers for input?

   Formally:

   _____

   _____

   _____

Informally:

_____

_____

_____

3. What is your organization doing now to ask for feedback from

Team members:

_____

_____

_____

Customers:

_____

_____

_____

4. What else will you do to ask for input from

Team members:

_____

_____

_____

Customers:

_____

_____

_____

STEP ONE: ASK FOR INPUT AND PUT IT TO USE (continued)

> *Communicate, communicate, communicate! Remember that communication is a "two-way street"—you want to listen and receive messages from employees and customers as well as talking or sending written messages.*

Communicating with Team Members

Keep your team up to date on changes, progress toward goals, and job expectations. That way, when you do ask for their input, they'll have a strong knowledge base to use as they give you feedback.

Mix formal and informal feedback methods to build an atmosphere where team members feel comfortable giving feedback. If you have regular staff meetings, add a short (5 to 10 minute) segment where you have a discussion question that asks for feedback or suggestions.

Sample questions include:

> *"How could we improve our . . . (specific process, detail involving work environment, or aspect of service)?"*

or

> *"What's the best way for us to solve XX problem?" Be sure to take notes and report back what you've done as a result of their feedback.*

Always be on the lookout for a chance to ask a team member one-on-one or in small groups, in the hall, on the shop floor, or at a company function, what they think about a procedure or how they'd solve a particular problem. Even if you don't have formal staff meetings, take a minute during brief pre-shift discussions or even in a newsletter or bulletin to ask a specific question soliciting their feedback.

Communicating with Customers

Keep your "service radar" turned on all the time for ideas from customers on how you can improve your products and service.

Ask for feedback in every way you can with

- ▶ **Simple written comment cards** or computer screens in very public locations

- ▶ **Short phone surveys** of recent customers

- ▶ **Staff members who ask customers open-ended questions** like "How was your stay/meal/experience with us?" and do simple tracking forms to follow up on answers

- ▶ **Include a simple survey** in customers' billing asking them to rate several aspects of your service and/or questions like "What could we do to serve you better?" or "How could we improve our product/ service?"

- ▶ **Focus groups** made up of customers or potential customers to ask targeted questions about how your business could improve

Be open-minded and listen when you ask for or receive input either from your team or customers. Being open-minded means suspending judgment long enough to consider the idea on its own merits, even if it's "off the wall" or a different way of looking at a situation. It doesn't matter where the idea comes from during the open-minded consideration.

Sometimes companies become defensive and try to explain away problems brought to their attention, as in the case of the complaint letter, discussed earlier. Those organizations miss an opportunity to acknowledge feedback and may overlook an area that needs improvement.

Let customers and employees know what you'll do with their ideas by responding to each one. Give them an immediate reaction whenever possible and tell them the "next step"—what you'll do with the idea.

STEP ONE: ASK FOR INPUT AND PUT IT TO USE (continued)

When you do use a suggestion or make a change as a result of customers' or employees' feedback, "advertise" the fact that you follow up on ideas. Do some internal or external "PR" with newsletters, ads, or other promotions that communicate the message, "Our customers/employees asked for _____ and we listened."

Asking for input is a major step toward building trust. Using the input whenever you can or explaining why if you can't use a particular idea is the key to making the communication process meaningful. You'll develop credibility of actions as you "do what you say you'll do."

STEP TWO: DO WHAT YOU SAY YOU'LL DO

Building trust helps you learn more about your operation because those around you will be more willing to share information with you. Success in this highly competitive business climate depends on your ability to be flexible enough to keep up with changes and new trends. If your team members feel that they can trust you, they'll be more likely to offer suggestions and pass on information to you. Your co-workers, in turn, will listen more closely and be more motivated to implement your ideas if they know that you mean what you say.

EXERCISE 17: What Kind of Example Are You?

Remember that trust depends on credibility of actions, including "doing what you say you'll do" and modeling the kind of behavior you expect from your employees yourself. To consider this step in our action plan for building trust, please complete both columns listed below:

The kind of example I set for my employees now:	The kind of example I'd like to set for my employees in the future:

STEP TWO: DO WHAT YOU SAY YOU'LL DO (continued)

Lead by Example

Your answers probably contain words like "honest," "considerate," "fair," "committed" and other terms describing the qualities of effective team members. Living by those words *yourself* is a surefire way to encourage others to trust you and to work well together.

Set an example by speaking and acting the way you'd like for your team members to treat your customers and each other. Insist upon open, honest, direct communication, and make sure that you follow your own rules.

For an example, remember the "Case of the Muddled Manager?" If you want your staff to greet your customers, then it's important for you to greet your staff. Otherwise, they will reject your suggestions because they won't believe that you actually do what you say everyone should do.

STEP THREE: DELEGATE EFFECTIVELY

Do your employees have the right to use their own judgment in offering low-cost amenities to customers—upgrades, free or discount coupons, pens or other simple "extras"? Do your team members have the ability and the freedom to make decisions to solve common customer problems without having to look for a manager every single time?

We're not talking about "giving away the store" here. Whether you use trendy words like "empowerment" or "self-directed work teams," the idea of giving others the responsibility and the accountability to make common daily decisions shows them you trust them and increases efficiency, morale, and customer satisfaction.

Trust and delegation go hand in hand. Delegation means giving team members the responsibility, authority, and accountability to make decisions on their own. Delegation doesn't mean that you, as their coach, abdicate the ultimate responsibility and accountability for your team's results.

Effective delegation comes from allowing your staff enough power to make decisions within whatever guidelines you set, making them accountable for their results, and establishing checkpoints along the way so that you can keep abreast of their progress.

EXERCISE 18: How Well Do You Delegate?

Answering the questions below will help you take a look at how much responsibility and accountability your team members have.

Please be as specific as possible with your answers, describing actual situations and/or guidelines.

1. What can your staff members offer to internal or external customers without having to ask management (that is, extras, options, extended deadlines, etc.)?

   _____

   _____

   _____

   _____

2. What other decisions could you allow your employees to make on their own without having to ask you for permission?

   _____

   _____

   _____

   _____

3. What other guidelines could you establish for your team that would help them make decisions on their own?

   _____

   _____

   _____

   _____

STEP THREE: DELEGATE EFFECTIVELY (continued)

Delegating effectively is one of the biggest challenges for American managers. It's hard to avoid either extreme—"dumping" projects on team members and walking away without any kind of follow up or "hovering" over team members every step of the way so that they end up feeling like you don't trust them to make a move without you.

> *Delegation is built on trust, not on abandonment or on micromanaging. It's hard for us to give up some control over work that we know we'll be accountable for in the long run.*

Striking a happy medium between too much and not enough delegation can be difficult. Both extremes hurt your efforts to build trust with your employees. Imagine a coach who sits way up in the stands to watch his or her team play on a small portable TV, making no contact with them. If you do that, you *abdicate instead of delegate.*

As your employees' coach, you need to take advantage of opportunities to give and receive feedback, something you can't do if you're too far removed. On the other side of the coin, players certainly don't want a coach who puts on a uniform and runs out on the field instead of keeping a coaching perspective. In that example, you're *interfering instead of delegating.*

Your team members will feel like you don't trust them enough to let them play the game themselves, with your guidance.

STEP THREE: DELEGATE EFFECTIVELY (continued)

EXERCISE 19: Rate Yourself

Where would you rate yourself on our delegation scale? Make a mark at the point which you feel represents your current delegation style as a coach.

Sitting in the stands with a portable TV

Putting on a uniform and running out on the field

⟵————————————————————⟶

An effective coach would mark somewhere in the middle between the two extremes.

What delegation is and what it isn't:

Delegation is:

- Built on trust

- Transferring a degree of power and accountability

- "To authorize and send (a person) as one's representative"—*The American Heritage Dictionary*

Delegation isn't:

- Micromanaging

- Totally giving up accountability

- Seagull management (that is, "Fly in, make a lot of noise, dump on everyone, and fly out")

Research has shown that many of the leadership qualities employees rate as being the most important relate to delegation and trust. *Encouraging* and *developing* your team members' skills comes from delegating effectively to them, with appropriate support and accountability. Trusting employees enough to let them assume responsibility for their actions, including the risk that they may fail, helps your team members learn and grow.

To delegate effectively, incorporate some of the basic concepts related to trust:

1. **Start small by sharing the load in daily tasks.** If you're uncomfortable with delegating, realize it and concentrate on changing your behavior.

2. **Be specific when you explain a task** or project which you're delegating.

3. **Use our "guidelines for giving feedback"** to catch others doing something *correctly* as well as helping them to improve.

4. **Don't micromanage.** How would you feel if someone looked over your shoulder all the time?

5. **Be available for questions.** Don't abdicate responsibility for the task/project and wait for someone to fail.

6. **Schedule regular "milestone meetings"** to check progress and deadlines.

7. **Don't just delegate tasks you don't like.** Remember that by delegating, you're helping your team members develop their own skills. Delegation helps you develop "credibility of actions" and trust.

STEP THREE: DELEGATE EFFECTIVELY
(continued)

Guidelines for Giving Feedback:

- **Be specific.** Avoid general statements like "Good job" or "That's wrong" unless you follow with a more specific comment. Tell the person what they did or didn't do well so that they know what to do next time. That's what good coaches do!

- **Talk with employees right away!** Don't let feedback get stale—it loses its punch.

- **Talk about what they did,** not who they are. Focus on job-related behavior. "You're nice" isn't an effective feedback statement by itself. "Thanks for being patient with that upset customer" targets the behavior you want to reinforce.

Trusting your team members enough to delegate to them is a vital business strategy. We're working harder and harder with our organizations demanding more and more productivity from us every day.

> *How can we possibly get all the work done and plan for future growth if we don't delegate to our employees by explaining projects or guidelines clearly and establishing checkpoints?*

Our team members will never be able to learn new skills and take responsibility if we don't trust them enough to allow them to make as many decisions as possible on their own without being forced to check with us every single time.

EXERCISE 20: Getting Started on Delegating

This exercise is designed to help you apply our information on delegation and trust to your own position. You will need to explain clearly to your staff member what you expect him or her to do regarding the task or project, including timeframes and checkpoints.

1. **Delegate a routine task that you do well (for example, scheduling, analyzing a report, reviewing records) to someone else.**

   What specific task or project will you ask someone else to do for you within the next week?

   _____

   _____

   _____

   _____

   To whom will you delegate that task or project?

   _____

   _____

   _____

   _____

   What will you say to explain that task or project to your staff member?

   _____

   _____

   _____

   _____

STEP THREE: DELEGATE EFFECTIVELY (continued)

2. **Follow up with your employee to check progress. Avoid the two extremes: micromanaging or ignoring the project until the completion date!**

   What milestones or checkpoints will you establish together?

   _____

   _____

   _____

   _____

Give your staff member feedback on his/her progress. Be just as careful to reinforce what's going well along with giving corrective feedback if necessary.

SUMMARY

The challenge, now, is to make your action plan "come alive." That's where the real work starts. As a leader, you establish and encourage positive relationships within and outside your company.

Positive relationships are grounded in trust. It's easy to read *Building Trust for Business Success* and say "Oh yeah, I'll do that" or "That doesn't sound too hard." Sometimes, putting these strategies into effect becomes very difficult. Here is a checklist to help you keep from backsliding.

You might want to freshen up on the concepts in this book, if you find that you:

- Ask your staff members for suggestions and don't want to use their ideas

- Promise to review a team member's project and get delayed

- Don't agree with an employee's "judgment call," even when the person went "by the book"

- Receive a customer complaint that you think is totally unjustified

It's during these challenges that it's crucial for you to remember that it's up to *you* to support and encourage an atmosphere of trust with your employees and your customers.

Find Someone You Can Trust

Trust is an integral part of business success. You can't expect people to trust you if you don't trust anyone else yourself.

The first step, then, to building trust with co-workers, is to find someone else at work, preferably in your department, whom you can trust. Although trusting a team member (or the whole team) may seem like a tremendous risk, a workplace without any trust is inefficient, expensive, and much less productive. Trust directly affects the bottom line.

SUMMARY (continued)

Teamwork involves two or more people working together toward common goals. To work together effectively, team members must trust each other. Teamwork and trust are not easy. We've seen all the "yabuts" we can come up with as obstacles.

Remember the questions you've asked yourself as you read this book: "What does this mean for me? How can I use these ideas to build trust back on the job?"

If you've done the exercises and the action plan, you've accomplished our objectives of:

- Defining trust for your own work environment.

- Determining how trust means business as a marketing tool and as a strategy to improve productivity, increase commitment, and help decrease turnover.

- Developing strategies for building trust back in your organization.

Trust is a key strategy that means success for your workers, your customers, and your company. The building blocks of success come from TRUST.

Remember, to succeed you've got to:

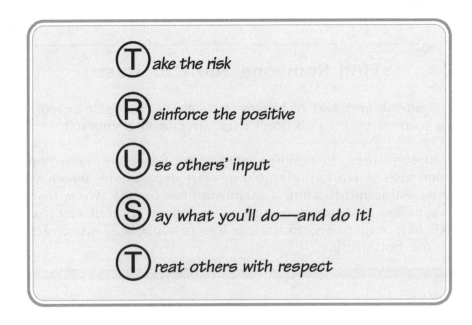

T ake the risk

R einforce the positive

U se others' input

S ay what you'll do—and do it!

T reat others with respect

NOTES

NOTES

NOW AVAILABLE FROM
CRISP PUBLICATIONS

Books • Videos • CD Roms • Computer-Based Training Products

If you enjoyed this book, we have great news for you. There are over 200 books available in the *50-Minute*™ Series. To request a free full-line catalog, contact your local distributor or Crisp Publications, Inc., 1200 Hamilton Court, Menlo Park, CA 94025. Our toll-free number is 800-442-7477. Visit our website at http://www.crisp-pub.com.

Subject Areas Include:

Management

Human Resources

Communication Skills

Personal Development

Marketing/Sales

Organizational Development

Customer Service/Quality

Computer Skills

Small Business and Entrepreneurship

Adult Literacy and Learning

Life Planning and Retirement

CRISP WORLDWIDE DISTRIBUTION

English language books are distributed worldwide. Major international distributors include:

ASIA/PACIFIC

Australia/New Zealand: In Learning, PO Box 1051, Springwood QLD, Brisbane, Australia 4127   Tel: 61-7-3-841-2286, Facsimile: 61-7-3-841-1580
ATTN: Messrs. Gordon

Singapore: 85, Genting Lane, Guan Hua Warehouse Bldng #05-01, Singapore 349569   Tel: 65-749-3389, Facsimile: 65-749-1129
ATTN: Evelyn Lee

Japan: Phoenix Associates Co., LTD., Mizuho Bldg. 3-F, 2-12-2, Kami Osaki, Shinagawa-Ku, Tokyo 141   Tel: 81-33-443-7231, Facsimile: 81-33-443-7640
ATTN: Mr. Peter Owans

CANADA

Reid Publishing, Ltd., Box 69559-109 Thomas Street, Oakville, Ontario Canada L6J 7R4.   Tel: (905) 842-4428, Facsimile: (905) 842-9327
ATTN: Mr. Stanley Reid

Trade Book Stores: *Raincoast Books,* 8680 Cambie Street, Vancouver, B.C., V6P 6M9   Tel: (604) 323-7100, Facsimile: (604) 323-2600
ATTN: Order Desk

EUROPEAN UNION

England: *Flex Training,* Ltd. 9-15 Hitchin Street, Baldock, Hertfordshire, SG7 6A, England   Tel: 44-1-46-289-6000, Facsimile: 44-1-46-289-2417
ATTN: Mr. David Willetts

INDIA

Multi-Media HRD, Pvt., Ltd., National House, Tulloch Road, Appolo Bunder, Bombay, India 400-039   Tel: 91-22-204-2281, Facsimile: 91-22-283-6478
ATTN: Messrs. Aggarwal

SOUTH AMERICA

Mexico: *Grupo Editorial Iberoamerica,* Nebraska 199, Col. Napoles, 03810 Mexico, D.F.   Tel: 525-523-0994, Facsimile: 525-543-1173
ATTN: Señor Nicholas Grepe

SOUTH AFRICA

Alternative Books, Unit A3 Micro Industrial Park, Hammer Avenue, Stridom Park, Randburg, 2194 South Africa   Tel: 27-11-792-7730, Facsimile: 27-11-792-7787
ATTN: Mr. Vernon de Haas